DIESEL TUGS
A Colour Portfolio

David L. Williams & Richard de Kerbrech

Ian Allan
PUBLISHING

Title page: This view of a group of South Shields towage and other marine craft on the buoys, shows Ridley's *Maximus* (nearest) alongside a quartet of old steam tugs. From the left, they are the *Gt Emperor*, the *Eastsider* and *Plover* with another unidentified France Fenwick steam tug beyond. The 171-gross-ton steam tug *Gt Emperor* had two-cylinder compound engines. Built in 1909 by J. T. Eltringham of South Shields for John Dry Steam Tugs, she transferred to France Fenwick in 1944 and was scrapped in 1959 at Kings Yard, Gateshead. Lawson-Batey's *Eastsider* was a 175-gross-ton, triple-expansion steam tug constructed in 1924. Oldest of the three identified tugs is her Lawson-Batey fleetmate, the compound-engined *Plover* built in 1881 by J. Reid & Co, Port Glasgow, as the *Fylde* for the Lancashire & Yorkshire Railway and London & North Western Railway companies. Lawson-Batey purchased her in 1909. Having been broken up at Gateshead by C. W. Dorkin & Co from 1957, her presence here helps to date this Tyneside scene. The nameplate of the 'Algerine'-class mine-sweeping sloop HMS *Albacore* (J101), constructed by Harland & Wolff in 1942, can be seen at the right, while the oil tanker in the background is the 21,178-gross-ton Norwegian-flag *Samuel Ugelstad*. *Kenneth Wightman*

First published 2006

ISBN (10) 0 7110 3117 7
ISBN (13) 978 0 7110 3117 3

© Ian Allan Publishing Ltd 2006

Published by Ian Allan Publishing

an imprint of Ian Allan Publishing Ltd, Hersham, Surrey KT12 4RG.
Printed in England by Ian Allan Printing Ltd, Hersham, Surrey KT12 4RG.

Code: 0605/B1

Visit the Ian Allan Publishing website at www.ianallanpublishing.com

Explanatory Notes

Preceding each caption or group of captions is a block of technical and date information relating to the named and featured tug or tugs. The layout of this information is as follows:

The tug's name (month and year built); former names (with the year in which the name changes occurred); the tug's owners; the tug's vital statistics: tonnage, length and beam in feet and inches (with the equivalent metric values); the tug's builders and shipyard location; the engine installation, the engine builders and, where known, the horsepower output.

Abbreviations

The following abbreviations have been adopted throughout:

2SA	Two-stroke single acting
4SA	Four-stroke single acting
bhp	brake horsepower
cyl	cylinders
fld	full load displacement, tonnage
ft	feet
grt	gross registered tonnage
ihp	indicated horsepower (a calculated or notional horsepower, nominally reckoned as 87% of brake horsepower)
in	inches
loa	length overall
m	metres

Acknowledgements

Bob Aspinall, Museum in Docklands; John Barrett, IoW Branch of the World Ship Society; John Bartlett, World Ship Society Central Record; David Clark; Justin Donald, Lloyd's Marine Intelligence Unit; David Hornsby; Jim McFaul, World Ship Photo Library; Don Smith; David Sowdon, World Ship Society Warship Information Service; Allison Wareham, Royal Naval Museum, Information Services, HM Naval Base, Portsmouth; Edward Wilson; Port of London Authority; Southampton Central Library — Maritime & Special Collections.

Introduction

This celebration in pictures of diesel tugs in Britain's inshore waters continues the story from the author's previous book *Steam Tugs: A Colour Portfolio* (Ian Allan Publishing, 2002). Based on the Kenneth Wightman collection, the pictures are a marvellous record of British shipping and UK port life in its heyday — a veritable trip down memory lane!

The marine internal combustion engine was first introduced around 1908 when four Russian-registered motor tankers were built for service on the Caspian Sea. Four years later, when the East Asiatic Company's *Selandia* made her maiden voyage from Copenhagen to Bangkok, the event attracted much greater international interest in this new form of marine propulsion. Installed aboard her was a Burmeister & Wain power plant derived from the original concept patented in 1893 by the German engineer Rudolf Diesel.

So successful was the *Selandia* and her later fleetmates, as well as other contemporary oil-engined vessels, that the internal combustion system was rapidly adopted for an increasing number of new craft and by 1914 some 300 motor vessels had been constructed. Although the steam turbine and the steam reciprocating engine remained the preferred option for certain applications, it was not long before diesel engines were being installed aboard a wide variety of ship types: cargo vessels, tankers, submarines, passenger liners and, ultimately, tugs.

It is not known for certain when the first motor tug was commissioned but by the 1950s the transition from steam-powered to oil-driven tugs was well under way; the advantages of fuel economy, a greater power-to-weight ratio, with reduced machinery spaces, plus near immediate operational availability were powerful incentives to towage operators. In the days of steam, tugs had either to raise steam prior to commencing work or remain under steam for long periods, wastefully consuming fuel and necessitating an appropriate level of crew accommodation, which imposed both heavier labour and operating costs on tug owners. Not surprisingly, some of the more recently commissioned steam tugs and even some quite elderly vessels were converted to diesel propulsion.

According to their type, diesel tugs were of comparable size to their steam equivalents, but the elimination of accommodation spaces permitted the installation of larger engine plants, giving them greater horsepower and, thus, heavier bollard pull rates.

Just as crew numbers on diesel tugs fell, so the overall numbers of tugs in each port also began to decline. Fewer, more powerful, tugs were required to do the equivalent amount of work. Furthermore, this was a time of accelerated change in shipping trades in general, which was leading to a lower demand for towage services. Larger vessels of greater capacity were appearing for all categories of operation, from ferries to oil tankers and from cargo ships to liners; break-bulk cargo handling was giving way to containerisation, all reducing the number of shipping movements, and an increasing number of ships were being fitted with bow and side thrusters, allowing their manoeuvrability in port to be controlled from the bridge. So, unlike the docks setting of a decade earlier, there were fewer vessels to be seen in general. No more the multitude of bustling coastal and river craft or the host of inbound and outbound cargo vessels headed by tugs that had once been typical of most British ports.

The pictures in this book reveal the harbours and docklands during this period of transition, an early manifestation of the massive changes that have inexorably altered the UK port scene for ever. Many of the scenes recorded no longer exist or have been developed beyond recognition as modern maps of the great tidal rivers of the UK will reveal. Once well-known landmarks and port features have disappeared under redevelopment schemes as the juggernaut of progress has rolled on, sweeping away old established cargo practices, port industries and communities, and shipping business in general.

It is fitting here to repeat some of the notes regarding the various tug types, many of which are featured in these pages, as well as to provide some explanation of the descriptions of the diesel engines installed aboard them.

In keeping with long-established towage practices, the four principal types of tug remained in use during the emergence of the diesel-engined variety, namely ocean salvage tugs, ship towage tugs, river or craft towage tugs and tender tugs. In Royal Navy parlance, the first two categories are more or less designated as fleet or sea-going tugs and harbour tugs. As far as possible, most of these types of tug are illustrated in the pages that follow. In parallel with the expanding adoption of diesel power, the roles of towage craft gradually became more diverse or specialized: for instance, fire-fighting tugs, coastal service tugs working in close conjunction with offshore oil and gas operations have been introduced and, most recently, tractor tugs — double-ended ship towage craft which can work as both 'pushers' (or 'nosers') and 'pullers'.

Tractor tugs have added a new dimension to ship handling, proving themselves to be especially valuable in the close confines of enclosed dock systems. With them, all towing is done from right aft where a towing winch and massive fairlead are located. Towing from this position considerably increases safety, making it virtually impossible for the tug to be capsized by the ship — the traditional ship-handling hazard.

For the most part, the diesel engines installed aboard tugs are, by necessity, of a simple arrangement in order to ensure reduced maintenance and trouble-free operation. The majority of the earlier diesel tugs were single-engined and single fixed-pitch screw vessels. Similarly, diesel tug engines are invariably of the single-acting type, where ignition occurs only at one end of the cylinder, rather than double-acting, where it occurs at either end of the cylinder. Likewise, for simplicity, the majority of tug diesel engines are two-stroke rather than four-stroke. Engines may have direct drive to the propeller shaft or there may be single-reduction or double-reduction gearing, for forward and reverse propulsion. Later diesel tugs were fitted with fluid couplings or flexible couplings. These are used between the engine and gearbox to dampen torque, to reduce the effects of shock loading on gears and the engine, and to cater for slight misalignments. The predominant engine configurations applicable to the tugs covered by this book are outlined on page 2, under 'Abbreviations'.

Many famous diesel engine manufacturers are featured, among them British Polar, Crossley, Ruston & Hornsby, Lister Blackstone, Burmeister & Wain, Atlas, Werkspoor, Mirrlees, Deutz and MAN (Maschinenfabrik Augsburg-Nürnberg), to name the more prominent, many having now disappeared as the result of mergers and takeovers.

Propulsion efficiency on diesel tugs has benefited from the introduction of Kort nozzles (ducted propeller units, some with aerofoil vanes permitting the traditional rudder to be dispensed with), Voith-Schneider units (cycloidal propellers placed at the bottom of the hull which function like a feathered paddle wheel), controllable pitch propellers (the blades of which can be rotated individually on their axis to suit varying conditions, permitting the elimination of reverse gearing) — sometimes described as variable-pitch propellers — and finally directional propellers (pivoting or rotational units with integral rudder and screw).

The dramatic changes that affected tugs and tug operation through the 1960s and 1970s were, likewise, mirrored in the story of UK tug ownership in this period. Amalgamations, takeovers and the formation of operating consortiums resulted in the disappearance of many famous towage business names, a process which witnessed, simultaneously, numerous changes to company colour schemes as well as the disappearance of well-known styles of nomenclature. Perhaps most pronounced was the rise of the Alexandra Towing and Cory Ship Towage empires. Alexandra Towing absorbed the Liverpool Screw Towing & Lighterage Company, North West Tugs, J. H. Lamey Ltd and London Tugs Ltd. Cory's took over R. & J. H. Rea Ltd and the Rea Towing Company Ltd. As rationalisation has continued, neither the Alexandra nor Cory concerns exists independently any longer.

Besides presenting a selection of wonderful vintage photographs of British tugs, this book also contains views of a small number of contemporary foreign diesel-powered tugs making calls at UK ports. While the majority of the pictures have come from the Wightman collection, in order to provide readers with a balanced coverage of diesel tugs based all around the UK, some images taken by other photographers have been included. The source of origination is noted in each case.

David L. Williams and Richard P. de Kerbrech
Isle of Wight, February 2006

ALNWICK
(10/1955) France Fenwick Tyne & Wear
119grt; 93ft 4in (28.44m) loa x 25ft 3in (7.70m) beam
P. K. Harris & Sons, Appledore
Vee Oil 2SA 12-cyl by General Motors Corp, USA:
1,080bhp

The France Fenwick motor tug *Alnwick* forges her way up river on the Tyne in a gale. She was one of a quartet of new diesel-powered craft built for the company in the 1950s. The others were the *Ashbrooke*, *Bamburgh* and *Marsden*. Their engines were reconditioned General Motors units originally constructed during World War 2. The streamlined Fred Olsen ferry *Blenheim* can be seen in the background, left. Of revolutionary design for the time, she and a sister vessel, the *Braemar*, were placed on the Bergen to Newcastle route in 1951. *Kenneth Wightman*

ASHBROOKE

(7/1955) France Fenwick Tyne & Wear — Tyne Tugs
119grt; 93ft 4in (28.44m) loa x 25ft 3in (7.70m) beam
P. K. Harris & Sons, Appledore
Vee Oil 2SA 12-cyl by General Motors Corp, USA:
   1,080bhp

One of the three sisters of the *Alnwick*, this is the *Ashbrooke*, photographed from the deck of the SEGB collier *Southwark*. Of welded construction and modern styled, these tugs featured an enclosed bridge and a combined funnel and mast structure. Unlike the *Alnwick*, which is shown carrying her owner's original colours with distinctive anchor emblem, the *Ashbrooke* has her funnel painted in the red and black colours of Tyne Tugs, a consortium formed in 1960 by the France Fenwick, Lawson-Batey and Ridley towage concerns. She is seen passing the Bergen Line terminal at the Commissioners Quay, North Shields. Alongside can be seen the stern end of the Bergen cargo ship *Astraea*, an ice-strengthened vessel of 3,190 gross tons and 313ft (95.40m) overall length. The *Ashbrooke* was sold to Orchid Maritime Co of Colombo, Sri Lanka, in 1984 and renamed *Gigas*. She remained classified with Lloyds Register until November 1986. *Kenneth Wightman*

GEORGE V

(1/1915) France Fenwick Tyne & Wear — Tyne Tugs
217grt; 114ft (34.75m) loa x 24ft 7in (7.50m) beam
J. P. Rennoldson & Son, South Shields
Oil 2SA 12-cyl by General Motors Corp, USA

Built as a steam tug in January 1915, the France Fenwick tug *George V* was converted to diesel propulsion in August 1954, at the same time receiving structural modifications that gave her a more modern appearance. Like the newly built craft joining France Fenwick, she, too, received General Motors diesel plant that had been originally constructed in wartime and reconditioned prior to installation. The *George V* is seen here on the Tyne in October 1964 working on the 26,000 tons full load displacement RFA oiler *Tideflow* (A97), built in 1954 by J. L. Thompson & Sons, Sunderland. The *George V* was apparently transferred to Lavington International ownership some time during the 1960s, although Lloyd's Register continued to show her as a France Fenwick vessel until 1975, when she was no longer listed. *Kenneth Wightman*

IMPETUS
(7/1954) Ridley Tugs Ltd — Tyne Tugs
141grt; 97ft 2in (29.61m) loa x 22ft 5in (6.83m) beam
Mutzelfeldtwerft GmbH, Cuxhaven
Oil 4SA 6-cyl by Klöckner-Humboldt-Deutz, Cologne:
    750bhp

Ridley Tugs' *Impetus*, here seen in Tyne Tugs colours, was the first diesel-powered tug to operate on the Tyne. Having cost her owners £53,240 when built, she was sold to J. Johannsen & Son Schleppschifffahrt, Lübeck in 1984 for £38,000. Renamed *Joachim*, she was later sold on twice more: to Niels Hendriksen, Denmark, in 1984 when she was renamed *Storesund* and then in November 1997 to the Madera Group, Panama, for whom she was given the name *Madera V*. She was last heard of in 2001, still in active service and operating in Bata, Equatorial Guinea, West Africa, where she was employed towing logs downriver to ocean-going ships for onward transportation.
Kenneth Wightman

MAXIMUS

(3/1956) Ridley Tugs Ltd — Tyne Tugs

141grt; 97ft 2in (29.61m) loa x 23ft 5in (7.14m) beam

Mutzelfeldtwerft GmbH, Cuxhaven

Oil 4SA 6-cyl by Klöckner-Humboldt-Deutz, Cologne:
    750bhp

Sister tug of the *Impetus*, this is the *Maximus* a lovely study of her in Tyne Tugs colours dating from July 1965. The *Impetus* and *Maximus* were both single-screw ship-handling tugs. The *Maximus* was sold in 1984 for £25,000 to McCann Tugs Ltd, Lowestoft. A further change of ownership followed in 1992 when she was sold on to the Paul Magnus Group for whom Lloyd's Register showed her as being in continuing active service in 2002. *Kenneth Wightman*

ROUGHSIDER

(5/1958) Lawson-Batey Tugs Ltd

Richard Dunston Ltd, Thorne

143grt; 92ft 6in (28.19m) loa x 23ft (7.01m) beam

Oil 4SA 6-cyl by Klöckner-Humboldt-Deutz, Cologne:
    750bhp

Here the *Roughsider* is seen with a black funnel, working in conjunction with a Lawson-Batey fleetmate, the triple-expansion steam tug *Joffre*, which dated from 1916. On the far side of the Tyne can be seen two oil tankers, an old Esso ship and, to the right, the *Clyde Crusader*, both very small by today's standards. The *Clyde Crusader* started life in 1954 as the *British Crusader*, built by Cammell Laird, Birkenhead. She measured 11,346 gross tons and had a deadweight capacity of 15,848 tons. After seven years under the BP Clyde Tanker Company houseflag, the *Clyde Crusader* reverted to her original name in 1964. *Kenneth Wightman*

QUAYSIDER

(9/1955) Lawson-Batey Tugs Ltd — Tyne Tugs
157grt; 97ft 2in (29.61m) loa x 23ft 5in (7.14m) beam
Mutzelfeldtwerft, Cuxhaven
Oil 4SA 8-cyl by Klöckner-Humboldt-Deutz, Cologne: 1,200bhp

WESTSIDER

(2/1964) Lawson-Batey Tugs Ltd — Tyne Tugs
151grt; 99ft 6in (30.32m) loa x 25ft 3in (7.70m) beam
Richard Dunston (Hessle) Ltd, Hessle
Oil 4SA 6-cyl by Klöckner-Humboldt-Deutz, Cologne: 1,000bhp

This cluster of Tyne Tugs, manoeuvring the new RFA fleet replenishment ship *Olynthus* (A122) in 1965, comprises the Lawson-Batey-owned *Quaysider* and *Westsider* along with the steam-powered *Joffre*. Just visible, tucked in behind them against the side of the RFA, is what appears to be Lawson-Batey's *Applesider*. Like the majority of ship-handling tugs that worked on the Tyne, the *Quaysider* and *Westsider* had four-stroke oil engines single-reduction geared to a single screw shaft. The *Westsider* was transferred first to Blyth, in 1983, and subsequently worked the River Wear and Sunderland docks until sold six years later to Clipper Cargoes Ltd, a Caribbean-based concern. Renamed *Towing Wizard* for TSA Tugs Ltd in 1984, the former *Quaysider* is now based at Leigh-on-Sea, Essex. *Kenneth Wightman*

LADY CECILIA

(1/1966) Humber Tugs Ltd, Grimsby
198grt; 106ft 3in (32.39m) loa x 29ft 8in (9.05m)
  beam
Appledore Shipbuilders Ltd, Appledore
2 x Oil 4SA 7-cyl by Ruston & Hornsby, Lincoln:
  850bhp

LADY THERESA

(1/1988) Howard Smith (Humber) Ltd
156grt; 79ft 9in (24.31m) loa x 25ft 4in (7.73m)
  beam
Cochrane & Sons, Selby
2 x Oil 4SA 6-cyl by Ruston Diesels, Newton-Le-
  Willows: 1,900bhp

These views show two generations of Humberside tugs. Above is the *Lady Cecilia*, an Immingham-based craft built originally for J. H. Pigott & Son Ltd, Grimsby, but here seen wearing Humber Tugs colours with the distinctive blue burgee on the funnel. Below, with a completely different livery, is the *Lady Theresa* which, at the time of her construction, was the third Humber tug of that name since 1962. Originally ordered for Humber Tugs (the restyled Pigott concern, which had been absorbed by the parent company of United Towing in 1964), the *Lady Theresa* is shown here painted in the livery of Howard Smith Towage. During 1987 this Australian concern acquired a controlling interest in the umbrella organisation which had owned Humber Tugs and United Towing since 1978, the North British Maritime Group. Seen assisting a Russian cargo vessel, the *Polotsk*, she has been included here as an example of the more recent development of the modern diesel-powered ship-handling tug. A distinctive feature is her control cabin, which has taken the place of the traditional bridge structure.
Both: Don Smith

FOREMAN

(6/1959) United Towing Company, Hull
227grt; 107ft 2in (32.66m) x 26ft 8in (8.12m) beam
Cook, Welton & Gemmell, Beverley
Oil 4SA 8-cyl by Ruston & Hornsby, Lincoln: 1,030bhp

A visitor to the Thames, the United Towing Company's *Foreman*, photographed in March 1966, was the company's first sea-going motor tug. With her tall, slim funnel, she retains the general appearance of a steam vessel. Beyond her, in mid-channel, is the general cargo ship *Galatia*, a Liberian-flag vessel of 9,462 gross tons, discharging timber into lighters. The *Foreman* was sold to C. J. King & Sons (Tugs) Ltd of Bristol in 1972. *Kenneth Wightman*

AVENGER

(11/1962) Elliott Steam Tugs
293grt; 118ft 5in (36.09m) loa x 30ft 5in (9.27m) beam
Cochrane & Sons, Selby
Oil 2SA 9-cyl by British Polar Engines, Glasgow: 1,800bhp

One of the most powerful single-screw motor tugs on the River Thames, the Elliott Steam Tugs' *Avenger* is shown painted in her owner's original colours, prior to the adoption of new livery by the Ship Towage (London) consortium. This towage group, formed in 1950, comprised, besides Elliotts, both the Gamecock Tugs and William Watkins concerns. This port bow view was taken in April 1963, with river traffic in the distance. *Kenneth Wightman*

DHULIA
(8/1959) William Watkins
272grt; 113ft 7in (34.62m) loa x 28ft 9in (8.76m)
 beam
Henry Scarr Ltd, Hessle
Oil 2SA 8-cyl by British Polar Engines, screw:
 1,280bhp

Virtually identical to Gamecock Tugs' *Moorcock*, this is William Watkins' *Dhulia*, completed just two months earlier by the same shipyard. This rationalisation of design and new vessel acquisition across the London tug fleets was clear evidence of the growing collaboration that came into effect following the creation of Ship Towage (London) in 1950. In this view the *Dhulia* still sports her owner's original funnel colours. She is manoeuvring slowly towards the Royal Terrace Pier, Gravesend, with a timber ship passing beyond her starboard quarter, inbound for the Surrey Commercial Docks. *Kenneth Wightman*

HIBERNIA
(1/1963) William Watkins — Ship Towage (London)
293grt; 118ft 5in (36.09m) loa x 30ft 5in (9.27m) beam
Cochrane & Sons, Selby
Oil 2SA 9-cyl by British Polar Engines, Glasgow:
    1,800bhp

Sister tug to the *Avenger*, the *Hibernia* has, like the ___ four fire-fighting spray nozzles mounted on the large platform abaft her forem___ ___ inclined trunking extending upwards to the platform, between the two outer legs of the tripod structure, contains the crew access way to the platform, its handrails on eith___ ___ ust visible. The Tilbury Passenger Landing Stage is in the background. *K___ eth Wightman*

IONIA
(8/1960) William Watkins
187grt; 99ft 9in (30.40m) loa x 26ft 2in (7.97m) beam
Henry Scarr Ltd, Hessle
Oil 2SA 6-cyl by British Polar Engines, Glasgow:
    1,250bhp

On a misty winter's day, William Watkins' *Ionia* tows the Mitsui-OSK Lines cargo liner *Harunasan Maru* stern-first through the entrance lock of the King George V Dock. The picture shows her prior to the adoption of Ship Towage (London) colours.
The *Harunasan Maru* was built by Mitsui Zosen at Tamano in 1954 for the London service from Japan. A single-screw motor ship, she measured 6,890 tons gross with dimensions of 504ft (153.61m) length overall and 64ft (19.50m) beam.
Kenneth Wightman

MOORCOCK

(10/1959) Gamecock Tugs
272grt; 113ft 6in (34.59m) loa x 28ft 8in
(8.73m) beam
Henry Scarr Ltd, Hessle
Oil 2SA 8-cyl by British Polar Engines,
Glasgow: 1,280bhp

Built for Gamecock Tugs and wearing
that company's distinctive colours, the
single-screw ship-handling tug *Moorcock*
sits dead in the water off the Royal
Terrace Pier, Gravesend, 1965, with the
Tilbury power station in the distance,
awaiting instructions for her next tow.
The *Moorcock*, like her contemporaries,
was equipped with radar, one of several
technical advances introduced during the
late 1950s/early 1960s, in parallel with
the growing transition to motor
propulsion. *Kenneth Wightman*

In the same vicinity — an ideal vantage
point for watching and photographing
Thames shipping and the tugs busily
manoeuvring in their working
environment — the *Moorcock* is seen two
years later, in 1967, with her funnel
repainted in Ship Towage (London)
colours. The elements of each of the
colour schemes of the constituent Ship
Towage concerns may be clearly seen on
the *Moorcock's* funnel: the red band of
William Watkins, the narrow pale blue
band representing Gamecock Tugs, the
chequered house flag of Elliott Steam
Tugs and the black top, common to all
three. *Kenneth Wightman*

Moving on another decade or more, the *Moorcock* is seen off Tilbury in her third colour transformation — this time the livery of Alexandra Towing. Along with all the other vessels of the London Tugs group taken over in 1975 by Alexandra Towing, with the single exception of the *Sun XXIV*, which was sold to Southampton, the *Moorcock* remained active as a Thames tug. *Don Smith*

PLAGAL

(11/1951) Port of Londo[...]
159grt; 92ft 10in (28.29m) [...] [...]in
   (7.36m) beam
Henry Scarr Ltd, Hessle
Oil 2SA 4-cyl by Crossley Bros, Manchester:
   1,200bhp

The Port of London Authority, formed in 1909 to consolidate and manage jointly all the docks along the Thames previously owned by private companies, owned and operated a large tug fleet in its own right. The *Plagal* was one of a group of four large motor tugs introduced by the Port of London Authority in the early 1950s, the others being the *Plangent*, *Plateau* and *Platina*. Designated as Dock Tugs, they were more or less the same as Ship Handling Tugs but, within certain limits, could also perform River Tug duties, if required. Here the *Plagal* takes the strain on a line wrapped around the stern of the Norwegian cargo ship *Byklefjell*, with a second stern line about to be connected. Uniquely, as the only tug of her class to be so modified, the *Plagal's* original single engine was replace[...] by two new 1,190bhp Rolls-Royce engines, installed in 1968. Eighteen years later she was [...] by G&T Services, Barking Creek. *Kenneth Wightman*

PLANGENT
(12/1951) Port of London Authority
159grt; 92ft 10in (28.29m) loa x 24ft 2in (7.36m) beam
Henry Scarr Ltd, Hessle
2 x Oil 2SA 4-cyl by Crossley Bros, Manchester:
 1,200bhp

High and dry in the Harland & Wolff floating drydock in the Surrey Commercial Docks, is the motor tug *Plangent*, one of the sisters of the *Plagal* described on the previous page. Dating from October 1964, the photograph shows the *Plangent* with twin Kort nozzle propulsion units, their integral rudders clearly visible. The class of four tugs, of which the *Plangent* was the lead vessel, were built with twin fixed-pitch screws and it is believed that she was the only one of the four craft to be converted in this fashion. Kort nozzles gave enhanced manoeuvrability, a valuable asset in the restricted waters of the enclosed docks of the Port of London. The *Plangent* was sold to Greek interests in 1987 and renamed *Cerberus*. Kenneth Wightman

PLATOON

(1965) Port of London Authority
117grt; 87ft 7in (26.69m) loa x
  26ft 7in (8.10m) beam
Richard Dunston (Hessle) Ltd,
  Hessle
Oil 4SA 16-cyl by Blackstone &
  Co, Stamford: 1,600bhp

The *Platoon* was one of a second class of four motor-engined Dock Tugs commissioned by the Port of London Authority, fitted with a single Voith-Schneider propeller. Introduced during the mid-1960s, they were specially designed to tow vessels inside the enclosed London Docks into which the tugs of private companies were not permitted. Her three classmates were the *Placard*, *Plankton* and *Plasma*. Small but powerful, they featured an unusual design configuration, with a long foredeck and, in contrast to conventional tug design, a very small working area aft with the absence of strongback or towing winch. Their overall appearance did not convey the impression of a tug but that of a utility harbour craft. Here the *Platoon* has a stern line from the 6,209-gross-ton *Africa Palm*, of Palm Line, secured to her aft end. From 1991, the *Platoon* went through several changes of ownership. First she went to Alexandra Towing as the *Dhulia*, transferring to Howard Smith (London) Ltd under the name *Caswell* in 1994. She underwent an internal transfer in 1998, to Howard Smith (Humber) Ltd and was given the name *Lady Theresa*, a name with long towage associations on the Humber. In a final move, in 2001, the former *Platoon* was sold to George Parschauer, Oldenburg, and her name shortened to *Lady*. Don Smith

RANA
(1951) London Tugs Ltd
99grt; 80ft 3in (24.46m) loa x 21ft 6in (6.55m) beam
Cochrane & Sons, Selby
Oil by British Polar Engines, Glasgow: 750bhp

FOSSA
(3/1961) London Tugs Ltd
83grt; 86ft 2in (26.26m) loa x 21ft 11in (6.68m) beam
Henry Scarr Ltd, Hessle
Oil 4SA 8-cyl by Klöckner-Humboldt-Deutz, Cologne: 1,000bhp

Working together near the West India Docks in April 1974 are two former Gaselee & Son motor tugs, the *Rana* (to the left) and the *Fossa*. Gamecock Tugs acquired this pair, along with the 1958-built *Culex*, from Gaselee in 1965. Of the two, the *Fossa* was, like certain of the PLA motor tugs already described, something of a hybrid: she was designated as a Ship Handling Tug but limited in her scope. Her size suited both ship towage and river towage duties and her certificate restricted her to River Thames service. The *Fossa* was, in fact, the last tug to join the Gaselee & Son company prior to its disappearance through takeover in the mid-1960s. *Kenneth Wightman*

SUN XVIII

(2/1951) W. H. J. Alexander (Sun Tugs)
105grt; 88ft 2in (26.87m) loa x 22ft 1in (6.73m) beam
Philip & Son, Dartmouth
Oil 4SA 7-cyl Ruston & Hornsby by Vickers-Armstrong,
   Barrow-in-Furness: 1,400ihp

The first motor tug to join the Sun Tugs fleet, *Sun XVIII* takes the bow line from the Royal Mail Lines cargo vessel *Pardo* near the Royal Docks entrance, in readiness to tow her from her berth as she departs for South America. Built by Harland & Wolff, Belfast, in 1940, the *Pardo* had a two-stroke, double-acting Burmeister & Wain diesel engine. She measured 7,480 gross tons, and was 450ft (137.15m) long by 61ft (18.59m) beam. The *Sun XVIII* was renamed *Ecclesbourne* in 1975 when sold to A. & N. Vogel, London. Two years later she became the *Alexandros*, following purchase by General Hellas Ltd, Greece. *Kenneth Wightman*

SUN XIX

(10/1956) London Tugs Ltd
192grt; 107ft 2in (32.66m) loa
    x 25ft 11in (7.90m) beam
Philip & Son, Dartmouth
Oil 4SA 6-cyl by Ruston &
    Hornsby, Lincoln: 1,210bhp

Returning to base at the Royal Terrace Pier, the *Sun XIX* presents an attractive image of a modern-styled motor tug, with a typical Thames shipping scene as her backdrop. The second motor tug to join the W. H. J. Alexander fleet, the *Sun XIX* here carries the London Tugs (formerly Elliott) houseflag on her funnel band, signifying that the photograph was taken after 1968 when Sun Tugs joined the Thames towage consortium. In fact, the picture was taken in February 1970 and shows, beyond the *Sun XIX*, at the Tilbury Landing Stage, one of the Soviet-flag passenger liners of the *Ivan Franko* class which then maintained a transatlantic service between Leningrad, London, Southampton and Montreal. In mid-river, bound for the estuary, is the 8,992-gross-ton, single-screw motor tanker *Anina*, built by A/S Frederikstad MV in 1955 and completed as the *Stemdal*.
Kenneth Wightman

SUN XX

(5/1957) W. H. J. Alexander (Sun Tugs)
192grt; 107ft 2in (32.66m) loa x 25ft 11in (7.90m) beam
Philip & Son, Dartmouth
Oil 4SA 6-cyl by Ruston & Hornsby, Lincoln: 1,210bhp

VANQUISHER

(3/1955) Elliott Steam Tugs
294grt; 113ft 3in (34.52m) loa x 28ft 9in (8.76m) beam
Henry Scarr Ltd, Hessle
Oil 2SA 8-cyl by British Polar Engines, Glasgow: 1,900ihp

Two London tender tugs take the strain on the bow lines of the Union Castle intermediate mailship *Rhodesia Castle*, as they ease her into Tilbury Docks. They are Elliott Tugs' *Vanquisher* (furthest) and the *Sun XX*. The *Sun XX* had a passenger certificate for 77 passengers while the *Vanquisher* could carry up to 100 passengers. The *Rhodesia Castle* served on the round-Africa route to Durban and Dar-es-Salaam, along with the *Braemar Castle* and *Kenya Castle*. Philip & Son, the builders of the *Sun XX* and many other Sun tugs, was well known as a supplier of lightships to the Corporation of Trinity House.
Kenneth Wightman

SUN XXIV

(6/1962) W. H. J. Alexander (Sun Tugs)
113grt; 88ft 3in (26.90m) loa x 22ft 11in (6.98m) beam
J. Pollock, Sons & Co, Faversham
Oil 4SA 6-cyl by Mirrlees, Bickerton & Day, Stockport: 1,000 ihp

Working the Soviet-flag cargo ship *Kolpino*, a Leningrad-registered vessel of 3,247 gross tons and 335ft (102.10m) long by 47ft (14.32m) beam — last of a large class of utility vessels built for the Soviet Union and other Communist bloc countries — is the Sun Tugs motor tug *Sun XXIV*. The diesel engine of the *Sun XXIV* featured a flexible coupling drive and single-reduction reverse gearing to her single screw. By contrast, the *Kolpino*, built by Schiffswerft Neptun, Rostock, in 1958, had steam reciprocating engines exhausting through a low-pressure turbine. Following the takeover of London Tugs by Alexandra Towing in 1975, the *Sun XXIV* was transferred to Southampton, see page 49. *Kenneth Wightman*

SUN XXV
(1/1963) W. H. J. Alexander (Sun Tugs)
230grt; 116ft 1in (35.38m) loa x 28ft 5in (8.66m) beam
Philip & Son, Dartmouth
Oil 4SA 6-cyl by Mirrlees National, Stockport: 2,400 ihp

One of two large fire-fighting tugs, the other being the Sun *XXVI*, this pair were the largest motor tugs to be constructed for the W. H. J. Alexander company. They passed into the hands of the Alexandra Towing Company in 1975 along with the majority of the other Sun motor tugs, following their original owner's merger with Ship Towage (London) some six years earlier. Compared with the Elliott fire-fighting tugs *Avenger* and *Hibernia*, the *Sun XXV* carries her spray nozzles on two levels. *Kenneth Wightman*

SUN XXVI

(3/1965) W. H. J. Alexander (SunTugs)
230grt; 116ft 1in (35.38m) loa x 28ft 5in (8.66m)
  beam
Charles D. Holmes & Co, Beverley
Oil 4SA 6-cyl by Mirrlees National: 2,400 ihp

Sister tug to the *Sun XXV*, the *Sun XXVI* was however built by Holmes at Beverley rather than at the Philip yard at Dartmouth. The *Sun XXVI* is seen here assisting the Soviet-flag short-sea passenger vessel *Baltika* in Gravesend Reach. The turbo-electric *Baltika* was built in 1940 as the *Vyacheslav Molotov*. Measuring 7,494 gross tons and 445ft (135.63m) long by 60ft (18.29m) wide, she served on the Leningrad to London route from 1946, initially under her original name, along with the later-built *Estonia* and *Mikhail Kalinin*. An interruption to these duties occurred in 1960 when the *Baltika* conveyed Party Chairman Nikita Khrushchev to New York. Just prior to her demolition in 1987, she performed a similar role, taking Mikhail Gorbachev to Iceland for a summit with President Ronald Reagan. *Kenneth Wightman*

TAYRA
(8/1926) Gaselee & Son
106grt; 85ft 9in (26.13m) loa x 21ft 7in (6.58m) beam
Alexander Hall & Co Ltd, Aberdeen
Oil 2SA 5-cyl by British Polar Engines, Glasgow: 700bhp

One of the oldest motor tugs on the River Thames and the only example in this book of a tug in the colours of Gaselee & Son is the *Tayra* whose tall, thin funnel belies the fact that her propulsion machinery is of the internal combustion type. Aided by an unidentified tug at the bows, the *Tayra* takes the stern lines from the 10,723-gross-ton Blue Star cargo-passenger liner *Uruguay Star*, helping to ease her away from the quayside in the Royal Albert Basin. The *Uruguay Star* was one of four large, modern steamships built by Cammell Laird, Birkenhead, between 1947 and 1948 for Blue Star's London to Buenos Aires service. The *Tayra* was disposed of in 1966, the year after her owners were absorbed by Gamecock Tugs. *Kenneth Wightman*

VANQUISHER

(3/1955) Elliott Steam Tugs
294grt; 113ft 3in (34.52m) loa x 28ft 9in (8.76m) beam
Henry Scarr Ltd, Hessle
Oil 2SA 8-cyl by British Polar Engines, Glasgow:
    1,900 ihp

The *Vanquisher*, here seen in her original guise, was
the tender tug of the Elliott fleet, certificated to carry
100 passengers. She heads the cargo ship *Indian
Splendour* through the entrance lock of the Surrey
Commercial Docks, with a William Watkins steam tug
manoeuvring the stern. The Surrey Commercial Docks
were the centre for timber product movements through
the Port of London, comprising nine large docks
surrounded by timber sheds. There were also numerous
timber ponds to hold lengths of imported woods.
Owned by the India Steamship Company, the 9,409-
gross-ton *Indian Splendour* was built in 1957 by
Howaldtswerke AG, Hamburg. *Kenneth Wightman*

WATERCOCK

(6/1967) London Tugs Ltd
166grt; 100ft 9in (30.71m) loa x 25ft 8in (7.82m) beam
Richard Dunston (Hessle) Ltd, Hessle
Oil 4SA 8-cyl by Ruston & Hornsby, Lincoln:
    1,050bhp

Being the replacement for a 1923-built steam tug of the
same name, the *Watercock* was the last new tug to join
the Ship Towage group prior to its merger with
W. H. J. Alexander's Sun Tugs. She was virtually a
sister to the William Watkins-owned *Burma*, completed
the same year. Pictured on a bright winter's day in
December 1968, the *Watercock* heads downstream at
speed past the Landing Stage at Tilbury. Alongside at
the Landing Stage is another, unidentified, modern-
style motor tug.
Kenneth Wightman

ACCORD

(1958) Admiralty — Royal Maritime Auxiliary Service (RMAS)
760 tons fld; 154ft 11in (47.2m) loa x 35ft 1in (10.7m) beam
A. & J. Inglis, Pointhouse, Glasgow
4 x HAXM Oil engines by Paxman: 1,800bhp

The Royal Navy tug *Accord* (A90) was one of five sea-going tugs of the 'Confiance' class fitted with two 2.5m-diameter Stone Kamewa variable-pitch propellers. She was based throughout her service career at Chatham Dockyard where she is seen in this photograph. Typical of Navy tugs, she exhibits a high freeboard below her rubbing strake in this picture taken in June 1981. Placed in reserve in 1985, the *Accord* was sunk as a target on 14 June 1986.
World Ship Society

EXPELLER

(1942) ex *Bora* (1945) Admiralty — Royal Maritime
  Auxiliary Service (RMAS)
317grt; 127ft (38.70m) loa x 26ft 5in (8.05m) beam
Nobiskrug Werft GmbH, Rendsburg
Oil 8-cyl by Motorenwerke, Mannheim: 820bhp

A German war prize allocated to the UK by the Tripartite Commission, the *Expeller* (A183) was acquired by the Admiralty for service at Chatham, where she is seen in this photograph alongside another unidentified, small tug of the Royal Maritime Auxiliary Service. The *Expeller* remained at Chatham until 30 September 1968 when she was sold to Salvatori Bezzina, Malta, and renamed *Sabi*. After a further 28 years of commercial service in the Mediterranean, the *Sabi* was towed to Aliaga, Turkey, in September 1996 for breaking up. *Kenneth Wightman*

DHULIA
(8/1959) William Watkins
272grt; 113ft 7in (34.62 m) loa x 28ft 9in (8.76 m) beam
Henry Scarr Ltd, Hessle
Oil 2SA 8-cyl by British Polar Engines, Glasgow: 1,280bhp

Although not widely known these days, up until 1960 Sheerness was a major Royal Dockyard with plenty of naval movements, besides being a port for ferries and other commercial vessels. Although primarily served by their own Admiralty tugs, until the closure of the Dockyard, civilian companies like William Watkins could be called upon to augment the towage and manoeuvring of warships when required. The *Dhulia* went on to give over 23 years' service on the Thames and its environs, with a sequence of owners, the last being Alexandra Towing. This view shows the *Dhulia* in drydock at Sheerness during September 1964. In 1983 she was sold to Chara SA General Maritime Enterprises (Antwerp) for whom she was renamed *Dhulia S. Kenneth Wightman*

KEMSING
(7/1960) J. P. Knight Ltd
135grt; 92ft 7in (28.22m) loa x 24ft 11in (7.59m) beam
T. Buschmann, Hamburg
Oil 4SA 8-cyl. by MAN, Augsburg: 1,000bhp

The next seven photographs are part of a series taken by Kenneth Wightman on the Thames Estuary, at Sheerness, during September 1964 (except where stated otherwise).

To meet the growing Sheerness and Thames seaway traffic, the J. P. Knight tug fleet was expanded with a new generation of tugs during the late 1950s and early 1960s. No fewer than five modern tugs were commissioned in the 10 years from 1955 to 1965. Unlike her contemporaries, the *Kemsing* was ordered by Knight's from a Hamburg yard, still quite a radical move for the time. Fitted with a single controllable pitch propeller, she proved a versatile and powerful addition to the company's fleet, designed to perform coasting services in addition to harbour duties. Her distinctive Continental style of integral mast and funnel became the fashion for subsequent vessels ordered by J. P. Knight. Here the *Kemsing* is seen on standby at Sheerness. *Kenneth Wightman*

KENDAL
(1939) ex *La Robuste* (1964) J. P. Knight Ltd
228grt; 117ft 8in (35.86m) loa x 25ft 7in (7.8m) beam
Ziegler Frères, Dunkirk
Oil 4SA 8-cyl Werkspoor (by builder): 1,100bhp

This large tug was originally built for the French towage company Société de Remorquage et de Sauvetage du Nord (SRSN), entering service as *La Robuste* just prior to World War 2. To meet its expansion programme Knight purchased her in 1964 and renamed her *Kendal*. Apart from Sheerness harbour towage and other duties, she could also be called upon, because of her size and power, for coasting services and work on the Thames Estuary when traffic was busy. She is seen here off Sheerness during March 1965, showing her rather dated prewar design with two masts. *Kenneth Wightman*

KENLEY
(6/1958) J. P. Knight Ltd
246grt; 108ft (32.92m) loa x 28ft 5in (8.66m) beam
Lobnitz & Co Ltd, Renfrew
Oil 2SA 8-cyl by British Polar Engines, Glasgow:
   1,500bhp

This high-powered, single-screw tug came from the Scottish yard of Lobnitz & Co which was heavily involved in the construction of the final generation of steam reciprocating powered vessels, which included towage craft. Besides port and Thames Estuary towage duties, the *Kenley* was also fitted out as a fire-fighting tug with five nozzles, four atop the bridge and one abaft the funnel. This view of her, taken off Garrison Point, clearly shows her with her fire-fighting equipment. Also, note the plethora of rubber tyre fenders along her freeboard, essential equipment resulting in an appearance common to all tugs of that era. The *Kenley* was sold in February 1984 and towed to Milton Creek for breaking up by Luguria Marine. *Kenneth Wightman*

KENNET

(7/1965) J. P. Knight Ltd

278grt; 113ft 6in (34.59m) loa x 30ft 4in (9.25m)
 beam

Richards Shipbuilders, Lowestoft

Oil 2SA 8-cyl by Mirrlees National: 2,000bhp

The design of the *Kennet* was influenced by that of the earlier, German-built *Kemsing* of 1960, although, unlike her predecessor, she had a single fixed-pitch screw and could develop twice the horsepower of the previous vessel! The *Kennet* was transferred to Humber Tugs in the mid-1990s. In this view, taken in August 1978, the *Kennet* is moored on the buoys off Sheerness, Kent, alongside the *Kemsing*. *Kenneth Wightman*

KESTON

(3/1970) J. P. Knight Ltd
299grt; 117ft (35.67m) loa x 31ft 3in (9.53m) beam
Richards Shipbuilders, Lowestoft
3 x Oil 4SA 8-cyl by Lister Blackstone Mirrlees Marine,
  Dursley: 3,000bhp

This purpose-built tug replaced a 41-gross-ton namesake that had been in service with Knight's since 1940. Her three diesel engines were reduction geared to three Kort nozzles. The *Keston* was given a greater range than other tugs owned by the Knight company and was also capable of coastal work around the UK, excluding the west coast of Ireland and the Continent coastline between the River Elbe and Brest. Her other role was that of a fire-fighting tug and she was equipped with a fire hose nozzle on top of the fire pylon abaft the bridge. This photo shows the *Keston* on 6 August 1978 in the River Medway alongside the *Eurco Faith,* a 3,784-gross-ton Greek general cargo vessel belonging to the Mare Shipping Co of Piraeus. *Kenneth Wightman*

KESTREL

(1/1955) J. P. Knight Ltd
223grt; 102ft (31.00m) loa x 28ft 5in (8.66m) beam
J. Samuel White & Company, Cowes, Isle of Wight
Oil 2SA 8-cyl by British Polar Engines, Glasgow:1,150bhp

Unlike other tug operators, which have had long-standing
relationships with particular shipbuilders, J.P. Knight appears to
have followed a policy where no single yard was preferred for its
new tonnage. Instead, it contracted a different shipyard for each
new tug. This may have been governed by factors such as cost
versus design specification or the economic benefits of taking 'off
the peg' designs offered by specialist tug builders. As each Knight
tug was to all intents and purposes unique, it would seem that the
company must have tried them all. For the single-screw *Kestrel* the
company went to the Isle of Wight firm of J. Samuel White who
were not specialist tug builders but more a warship-oriented yard,
although it has to be said it was not Knight's first association with
White's. In the 1930s J. Samuel White built three motor tugs for
J. P. Knight Ltd: the *Kelpy* (1934), and the *Kathleen* and *Katra*
(1936). This shot shows the *Kestrel* hove to awaiting orders. Along
with fleetmate *Kenley*, the *Kestrel* was scrapped from February
1984 by Luguria Marine, Milton Creek. *Kenneth Wightman*

KEVERNE

(5/1960) J. P. Knight Ltd
247grt; 123ft (37.49m) loa x 28ft 5in (8.66m) beam
John I. Thornycroft, Southampton
Oil 2SA 8-cyl by British Polar Engines, Glasgow: 1,650bhp

This 1960-built tug followed the similar general design and layout
as the *Kemsing* and *Kennet*, with their combined funnel and mast
configuration and generally uncluttered appearance. However,
unlike the other two, the *Keverne* was a purpose-built fire-fighting
tug as well, with her three fire hose nozzles on the monkey island.
She had enhanced manoeuvrability as her single screw was
incorporated into a Kort nozzle. This, combined with her powerful
diesels, also made her a speedy vessel. In this picture of her, taken
during November 1964, the *Keverne's* fire-fighting equipment is
clearly displayed. *Kenneth Wightman*

FAITHFUL

(1958) Admiralty — Royal Maritime Auxiliary
    Service (RMAS)

710 tons fld; 473grt; 157ft 2in (47.91m) loa x
    59ft 10in (18.24m) beam, 30ft (9.14m) across the
    hull

Yarrow, Scotstoun

4 x Oil engines by Paxman, connected to 2 x electric
    motors each driving a paddle wheel: 2,000bhp

The *Faithful* (A85) was one of the 'Dexterous' class of seven Large Harbour Tugs, distinguished as being the only naval paddle tugs in the world having diesel-electric propulsion. They were specially designed for handling aircraft carriers, able to work close under the overhanging flight decks. Their independently operated paddle wheels made them very manoeuvrable within the confined spaces of dockyards. In this view, the *Faithful* manoeuvres alongside the 'Audacious' class aircraft carrier *Ark Royal* (R09) during the Silver Jubilee Fleet Review at Spithead in 1977. Her three strongbacks can be clearly seen. The *Ark Royal* survived for barely two more years, her name transferring to a new lighter carrier (R07) of the 'Invincible' class, completed in 1985. The *Faithful* was withdrawn from service on 4 September 1981 and laid up at Devonport. She left Devonport under tow on 12 April 1983, bound for Gibraltar, where, nine days later, she was sunk off the coast as a target ship. *Don Smith*

ATHERFIELD

(5/1956) Red Funnel Towage
246grt; 112ft (34.14m) loa x 29ft 7in (9.02m) beam
John I. Thornycroft, Southampton
2 x Oil 2SA 6-cyl by Crossley Bros, Manchester:
   1,340bhp

Launched on 14 March 1956, the *Atherfield* was the first motor tug to be commissioned by Red Funnel. The *Atherfield* and her later sister, *Culver*, were designed specially for fire-fighting duties at Fawley Oil Refinery in Southampton Water. Capable of delivering 3,000 gallons of water per minute, backed up by 6,000 gallons of 'Foamite', carried in two tanks, their fire-fighting equipment comprised six swivelling monitors and four double hoses. Like the majority of Red Funnel motor tugs at Southampton, the *Atherfield* and *Culver* were fitted with twin screws. Withdrawn from service in 1971, when the new *Gatcombe* and *Vecta* were placed on the Fawley station, the *Atherfield* was sold to J. D. Irving (Atlantic Towing Co) of Saint John, New Brunswick, Canada. She left Southampton, to cross the Atlantic, on 4 May 1971 and was renamed *Irving Hemlock* on arrival at her new home port. In the background of this view, taken off Hythe, are the tugs *Dunnose* (on the left) and *Ventnor*. *World Ship Society*

BROCKENHURST

(11/1964) Alexandra Towing Co Ltd
173grt; 103ft (31.40m) loa x 27ft (8.23m) beam
R. Dunston (Hessle) Ltd, Hessle
Oil 2SA 8-cyl by Crossley Bros, Manchester: 1,200bhp

The *Brockenhurst* was one of a second class of three new motor tugs introduced by Alexandra Towing for its Southampton operations in the mid-1960s, the others being the *Romsey* and *Ventnor*. Single-screw tugs, they were marginally less powerful than previous Alexandra motor tugs located at Southampton. Here, the *Brockenhurst* can be seen off Netley, in Southampton Water, with a fleetmate off her port side. At present owned by the Merseyside Maritime Museum, the *Brockenhurst* attended the Trafalgar Fleet Review off Spithead on 28 June 2005. *World Ship Society*

CALSHOT [I]

(1/1930) Southampton
City Council

702grt; 147ft 8in (45.00m)
loa x 33ft 1in (10.09m)
beam

John I. Thornycroft,
Southampton

2 x Oil 2SA 8-cyl by N. V.
Mach 'Bolnes',
Krimpen: 800bhp

As originally built for Red Funnel, the *Calshot* was fitted with triple-expansion steam engines driving her twin screws through single-reduction gearing. In 1964 she was sold to Port & Liner Services (Ireland) Ltd (a subsidiary of the Holland America Line) and renamed *Galway Bay*. She was then converted to her present diesel machinery and stationed at Galway.

Completed as a tug/tender with a capacity for 566 passengers for port work in Southampton and tendering of ocean liners moored in Cowes Roads, at peak holiday periods she was also frequently used on the Southampton to Ryde excursion service as a relief vessel. During World War 2 the *Calshot* was used on Admiralty service at Scapa Flow, tendering the warships based there. By 1944 she had returned to Southampton for D-Day operations. Thirty-four years of auxiliary and Red Funnel service were followed by a further 22 years on the west coast of Ireland. Then, during 1986, the *Galway Bay* was purchased by Southampton City Council on behalf of the Southampton Museums and returned to her old home port for preservation. In the photograph, taken in June 2005, she is seen at Berth 42, Southampton Old Docks, once more wearing her original name. As part of the restoration, she will be returned to her former exterior appearance including the erection of a replica of her original steamer funnel — a taller and narrower structure than the one seen here — kindly donated by Vosper-Thornycroft. Already the luxurious furnishings of her interior passenger spaces have been completely renovated. However, the *Calshot* will retain her oil engines, though whether they will ever be fired up again remains to be seen. *David Williams*

CALSHOT [II]

(3/1964) Red Funnel Towage
494grt; 139ft (42.36m) loa x 35ft 1in (10.70m) beam
John I. Thornycroft, Southampton
2 x Oil 2SA 8-cyl by Crossley Bros, Manchester:
    1,800bhp

Built for Red Funnel as a sister to the tug/tender *Gatcombe* of 1960 and as a replacement for the earlier *Calshot*, the twin-screw *Calshot* of 1964 had a certificate for 215 passengers. The design of the *Gatcombe* and *Calshot* was not unlike that of the later Offshore Rig Supply Vessels (ORSV) that came into operation in the 1970s and the former vessel in fact performed these duties for Shell (UK) Ltd from 1968 to 1969. Despite the decline in passenger shipping at Southampton, the *Calshot* maintained her tug/tender duties in the port until 1989 when she was sold to Dublin Bay Cruises and renamed *Tara II*. This fine view of the *Calshot* at Southampton, heading towards the Old or Eastern Docks, was taken in October 1970. *World Ship Society*

CHALE

(7/1965) Red Funnel Towage
254grt; 112ft 5in (34.17m) loa x 27ft (9.02m) beam
John I. Thornycroft, Southampton
2 x Oil 2SA 6-cyl by Crossley Bros, Manchester:
    1,340bhp

As a development of the earlier Red Funnel twin-screw motor tugs, the *Chale* differed slightly from her two half-sisters, *Dunnose* and *Thorness*, by having a completely enclosed bridge. She was the last tug to come from the Thornycroft yard at Woolston. Later (after the photograph shown here was taken), the *Chale* was fitted with fire-fighting equipment, mounted above her bridge and atop a tall, latticed tower structure, similar to that of the *Culver* (see picture on page 48). The *Chale* was sold out of the Red Funnel Towage fleet in the summer of 1986. *World Ship Society*

DUNNOSE

(6/1958) Red Funnel Towage

241grt; 112ft 1in (34.16m) loa x 29ft 9in (9.07m) beam

John I. Thornycroft, Southampton

2 x Oil 2SA 6-cyl by Crossley Bros, Manchester: 1,340bhp

Launched on 20 March 1958, the twin-screw *Dunnose* entered service with Red Funnel in June that year and served with them until 1980. Her design was based on that of the *Atherfield* class of motor tugs introduced from 1956. The main difference from her precursors was that she did not have a raised bridge, her wheelhouse being forward on the boat deck. She is seen here taking up station at the bow of Norddeutscher Lloyd's 21,514-gross-ton passenger liner *Europa* (ex *Kungsholm*) during a departure from Southampton for New York in September 1967. Thirteen years later the *Dunnose* was sold to J. D. Irving Ltd, New Brunswick, for whom she was renamed *Irving Willow*. *Kenneth Wightman*

FLYING KESTREL
(1976) ex *Karl* (1986)
FLYING OSPREY
(1976) ex *Cornelie Wessels* (1986) ex *Johanna* (1978)
Alexandra Towing Company
223grt; 97ft 2in (29.61m) loa x 30ft (9.15m) beam
Mutzelfeldtwerft GmbH, Cuxhaven
2 x Oil 4SA 8-cyl by Deutz with single-reduction drive

Both these vessels, sister tugs built originally for Continental operators, are designated 'tractor' tugs and have a bollard pull of 36 tonnes. They have twin directional propellers and their hulls are ice strengthened. Both were later sold on to Howard Smith Towage Ltd when Alexandra Towing ceased operations at Southampton in 1993. Subsequently, the *Flying Kestrel* was resold in 2001 and renamed the *Arion*, while the *Flying Osprey* was sold to Norwegian buyers in 2005. Here seen on standby during 1996, both tugs await orders. *Richard de Kerbrech*

GURNARD

(1961) ex *Aziebank* (1982) ex *Azie* (1973) Red Funnel
  Towage
161grt; 94ft 8in (28.86m) loa x 27ft 6in (8.39m) beam
NV Schps v/h H. H. Bedowes, Millingen, Netherlands
2 x Oil 4SA 8-cyl by Kon Mach Stork & Co NV:
  1,360bhp

Built in 1961 as the *Azie* for P. Smit Jnr of Rotterdam, this twin-screw tug became the *Aziebank* in 1973 when she was acquired for the Nieuwe Rotterdam Sleepdienst fleet. As such she came to Southampton during September 1982 as a demonstration of an innovative type of 'tractor' tug. Following resolution of problems with one of her propulsion units she was bought by Red Funnel and renamed *Gurnard*. Her twin diesel engines drive twin Voith propulsion units giving her greater manoeuvrability, especially in confined waters. During 1985 the *Gurnard* was sold to Alexander Towing Co, for service at Gibraltar, and renamed *Wellington*. Here she is seen freshly painted passing the Hythe Marina. *Richard de Kerbrech*

REDBRIDGE

(1995) Red Funnel Towage
399grt; 108ft 2in (33.0m) loa
    x 38ft 6in (11.73m) beam
Yorkshire Drydock Ltd, Hull
2 x Oil 4SA 9-cyl by Stork-
    Wartsila Diesel BV, Zwolle

Not only does the *Redbridge* perform as a port tug but she also has the facilities to double up as a fire-fighting tug with her directional high-power hose jets. This powerful omni-directional 'tractor' tug with a bollard pull of 45 tonnes was built at a cost of £3.5 million for Red Funnel Towage. As such she was among the last of a long line of tugs built for the company. She is included here for comparison with other earlier towage craft, as an example of the development of the design of the motor tug over the past 10 or so years. Her sturdy engines are double-reduction geared via flexible couplings to twin Voith-Schneider propulsion units.

In 2002 Red Funnel Towage was sold by Associated British Ports, which had acquired the Red Funnel Group some years earlier, to the Australian company Adsteam Marine Ltd (a derivative of the former Adelaide Steamship Co). This was done to permit the Red Funnel Group to concentrate on its ferry and road transport interests. Among the assets transferred to Adsteam Marine was the *Redbridge*, along with the *Vecta*, *Hamtun* and *Sir Bevois*. In the photograph the *Redbridge* is seen tending the small Greek liner *Orpheus* as she manoeuvres astern whilst departing on a cruise from Southampton on 20 August 1997. Although a lot smaller than the larger cruise ships that nowadays frequent Southampton, she still requires the *Redbridge's* services as she is an older liner without a bow thruster. *Richard de Kerbrech*

47

CULVER

(1956) Red Funnel Towage
246grt; 112ft 2in (34.14m) loa x 29ft 7in (9.02m) beam
John I. Thornycroft, Southampton
2 x Oil 2SA 6-cyl by Crossley Bros, Manchester;
   1,340bhp

A group of Southampton's motor tugs meets the liner *Uganda* on the occasion of her return to her home port on 9 August 1982 after her duty as a hospital ship in the South Atlantic during the Falklands War of that year. The traditional greeting to mark a special event — in this case a safe return — of operating her fire-fighting hoses in a salutary spray, is given by the Red Funnel tug *Culver* (left of picture). The same tribute is afforded to vessels making their maiden voyages, anniversaries of longevity and, sometimes, on their final departures from the port. At the right of picture is thought to be Red Funnel's motor tug *Chale*, dressed in bunting to celebrate the *Uganda's* arrival. Alongside the *Uganda* is Alexandra Towing's large (272-gross-ton) bluff-nosed tug *Victoria*, one of a pair with the *Albert*, which had entered service in 1972.
Richard de Kerbrech

SUN XXIV

(6/1962) Alexandra Towing Company
113grt; 88ft 3in (26.90m) loa x 22ft 11in (6.98m)
beam
J. Pollock, Sons & Co, Faversham
Oil 4SA 6-cyl by Mirrlees, Bickerton & Day,
Stockport: 1,000 ihp

Following her acquisition by Alexandra Towing from London Tugs in 1975, the *Sun XXIV* was repositioned at Southampton Docks where she is photographed assisting the Norwegian-flag cruise ship *Norway*, formerly the graceful CGT liner *France*, at one time the longest ship in the world. The *Sun XXIV* was purchased by Newhaven owners in 1992 and renamed *Kingston*. As for the *Norway*, she was towed from her lay-up berth at Bremerhaven in June 2005 to Port Kelang, Malaysia, on the Malacca Strait, ostensibly for a static role. At the time of writing, many fear that the 43-year-old passenger ship will subsequently be diverted to an Indian scrapyard. *Don Smith*

THORNESS

(3/1961) Red Funnel Towage
247grt; 112ft 5in (34.26m) loa x 30ft 2in
  (9.19m) beam
John I. Thornycroft, Southampton
2 x Oil 2SA 6-cyl by Crossley Bros,
  Manchester: 1,340bhp

The twin-screw *Thorness* was launched on 17 January 1961 as a sister to the *Dunnose* and was delivered two months later on 28 March, thus entering service during Red Funnel's centenary year. Each engine was single-reduction geared via flexible couplings to the screw shafts. The *Thorness* served at Southampton for 22 years until 1983. That year, she and the *Culver* were sold to J. D. Irving Ltd (Atlantic Towing) of Saint John, New Brunswick, in Canada. Preparations were made for the storage of extra fuel by both tugs in order for them to have the range for the Atlantic crossing, the work being carried out at the Camber in Portsmouth. Upon her arrival in Canada, the new owners of the *Thorness* renamed her *Irving Juniper*. The above view was taken from the deck of the Cunard passenger liner *Queen Mary* in June 1963. Taking the strain along with the *Thorness*, and to her left, is the earlier Red Funnel steam tug *Sir Bevois* (pronounced 'beevis' by locals). *Kenneth Wightman*

WELSHMAN

(1942) ex *Castle Peak* (1962)
    ex *Caroline Moller* (1954)
    ex *Growler* (1952) United Towing
    Company, Hull
1,120grt; 205ft (62.48m) loa x 38ft
    6in (11.73m) beam
Henry Robb, Leith
2 x Oil by Atlas & British (Polar):
    4,000bhp

Photographed in the River Fal, Cornwall, is the *Welshman*, a former wartime naval fleet tug. She was built as the second unit of the eight-vessel 'Bustler'-class, the first fleet tugs with diesel engines to be completed for the Admiralty. Up to 1963, the *Welshman* was the largest commercial tug on the British Register with a range of 17,000 miles at 14 knots, her owner being the principal operator of large, ocean-going salvage and towage craft under the Red Ensign. Despite her large size, the United Towing Company went on to own considerably bigger vessels than the *Welshman*, the largest and one of the most powerful being the 1971-built *Lloydsman* of 2,041 gross tons and 262.5ft (80.00m) long. This vessel had diesel engines producing 16,000bhp, driving a controllable pitch propeller in a Towmaster 17ft (5.2m) diameter Kort nozzle fitted with aerofoil steering vanes. No longer, in fact, a United Towing vessel when this picture was taken, the *Welshman* is seen laid up following the end of a five-year charter from the Admiralty. *Kenneth Wightman*

MARINIA
(1/1955) Overseas Towage & Salvage
392grt; 129ft 7in (39.49m) loa x 29ft 10in (9.09m) beam
Cook, Welton & Gemmell, Beverley
Oil 2SA 6-cyl by British Polar Engines, Glasgow: 960bhp

The large, single-screw fire-fighting and general purpose salvage tug *Marinia* was based at Milford Haven operating in the Bristol Channel area but also active, as contracted, all around the coast of the UK. Here she is seen in March 1963 on the buoy in an unknown anchorage with two other craft, the nearest being the barge GW66. The largest tug in the OTS fleet at that time was the 600-gross-ton *Britonia*, delivered in 1963, with a power output of 2,000ihp. The *Marinia* was sold to Selco (Singapore) Ltd in 1966 and renamed *Salvana*. *Kenneth Wightman*

POLGARTH
(4/1962) Cory Ship Towage Ltd
160grt; 94ft (28.65m) loa x 26ft 1in
  (7.95m) beam
Charles Hill & Sons Ltd, Bristol
Oil 4SA by Ruston & Hornsby, Lincoln:
  1,080bhp

The *Polgarth* was laid down for R. &. J. H. Rea Ltd, London, in September 1961 and launched just four months later, one of a pair — the other being the *Pengarth* — for operation in the Bristol and Avonmouth docks. Their four-stroke engine arrangement, single-reduction geared to a single fixed-pitch propeller gave them a creditable bollard pull of 14.5 tons. In 1970 the *Polgarth's* owners became Cory Ship Towage Ltd after that company absorbed the various Rea towing concerns, later restyled as Cory Towage. After 19 years with Corys, the *Polgarth* was sold to S. Evans at Garston for demolition but within a year she was resold to Divemex in South-West Wales who placed her under Honduran registry and renamed her *Oliver Felix*. Under this name she was chartered back to Cory Towage for two years. Two further sales then followed, to WAM (GB) Ltd of Carryduff, Belfast, in October 1995, and then to General Marine Ltd, Wapping, London, in March 1999. She was still in service at the turn of the millennium — not bad for a craft that had been destined for breaking up some 11 years earlier. *Don Smith*

FORMBY
(8/1960) ex *Weather Cock* (1970)
Alexandra Towing Company
159grt; 95ft 3in (29.03m) loa x 25ft 11in (7.9m) beam
Cammell Laird & Co, Birkenhead
Oil 4SA 6-cyl by Ruston & Hornsby, Lincoln: 1,066bhp

Completed as the last tug to be built for North West Tugs, the *Weather Cock* served the Mersey Estuary and the port of Liverpool out to its limiting seaward boundary of the Bar Lightship. When Alexandra Towing took over North West Tugs she was renamed *Formby*, following a nomenclature that commemorated docks in the Port of Liverpool. Here she is seen on 16 October 1976 sporting the Alexandra Towing livery, under way off the Gladstone Entrance. The *Formby* was lost in unusual circumstances in October 1981, along with two other of her former North West Tugs fleetmates, after she had been sold to Nicolas E. Vernicos, Greece, and renamed *Vernicos Alexia* — see the *Heath Cock* on page 56. *Jim McFaul*

FOYLEMORE

(8/1958) Johnson Warren Lines
208grt; 103ft 6in (31.54m) loa x
27ft 9in (8.46m) beam
W. J. Yarwood & Sons, Northwich
Oil 4SA 7-cyl by Ruston &
Hornsby, Lincoln: 1,270bhp

The *Foylemore* was built as one of a trio of small but powerful tugs of 22 tons bollard pull for Johnson Warren Lines, which was then part of the mighty Furness Withy Group, her sisters being the *Kilmore* and *Rossmore*. As built, they were used for harbour towage of the many Furness Withy vessels that had Liverpool as their main terminal. Laid down in July 1957, she was launched in April 1958 and entered service four months later. Purchased by the Rea Towing Company, Liverpool, in 1968, the *Foylemore* was renamed *Foylegarth* a year later. Subsequently, she passed into the ownership of Cory Ship Towage Ltd, with whom she remained until 1983. In that year she was sold to H. Pounds at Portsmouth for use at the Albert Johnston Quay to augment MoD tugs but within 12 months she had been traded again, to the Falmouth Towage Company, and renamed *St Budoc*. Here the *Foylemore* is seen towing Shaw Savill & Albion's *Doric* through the Gladstone-Hornby Lock into the River Mersey. The *Foylemore's* funnel is brightly painted in the Furness Withy colours, while the 10,674-gross-ton *Doric* with her twin five-cylinder Doxford opposed piston engines, was also part of the Furness Withy empire. *Kenneth Wightman*

HEATH COCK

(2/1958) North West Tugs Ltd
193grt; 102ft 2in (31.14m) loa x
   27ft 11in (8.51m) beam
Cammell Laird & Co, Birkenhead
Oil 4SA 6-cyl by Ruston &
   Hornsby, Lincoln: 1,088bhp

The *Heath Cock* was the first motor tug to be built for North West Tugs. One of a pair propelled by diesel engines, her sister was the *West Cock*. Their Ruston & Hornsby oil engines drove a single screw via a flexible coupling and single-reduction and reverse gears, developing a brake horsepower equal to that achieved by the company's earlier steam-driven tugs. The *Heath Cock* was transferred to the Alexandra Towing Company during 1966 and renamed *Collingwood* in 1970. Ten years later, she was sold to Greek interests and renamed first *Collingwood II* and then *Vernicos Barbara IV*. In convoy with the *Vernicos Georgis* (ex *Canada II*, ex *Canada*, ex *Pea Cock*) and the *Vernicos Alexia* (ex *Formby*, ex *Weather Cock*), she left the Mersey in October 1981 bound for the Mediterranean. In order to save fuel costs, the Greek owners decided that the *Vernicos Georgis* should tow her consorts for part of the voyage. However, off St David's Head, the towing vessel developed engine trouble and while stopped the tow line became fouled in her propeller. On 18 October 1981, with increasing winds, the three now adrift and helpless tugs were driven ashore near Solva, in St Brides Bay, where they were wrecked. Here the *Heath Cock* is seen in better times at the centre in a lock full of 'Cock' tugs, including *Game Cock V*, awaiting orders. *World Ship Society*

JOHN LAMEY
(1927) ex *Lady Elizabeth* (1957)
    ex *Geertruida XV*
J. H. Lamey Ltd, Liverpool
185grt; 100ft 8in (30.68m) loa x
    21ft 7in (6.58m) beam
Jonker & Stans, Hendrik-Ido-
    Ambacht, Netherlands
Oil 2SA 8-cyl by Crossley Bros,
    Manchester

Originally built for the South African Railways as the steam-powered *Geertruida XV*, this tug had a long career at Cape Town before joining J. H. Lamey Ltd of Liverpool for port and harbour towage. She was rebuilt and re-engined with reconditioned 1943-constructed Crossley diesel engines, after which she entered service as the *John Lamey*, becoming the first motor tug in Mersey service. In 1967, when 40 years old, she was sold on to G. R. Walker of Kingswear, Devon, and renamed *Harry Sharman*. As such she was sunk off the Culver Cliff at the extreme eastern point of the Isle of Wight during a gale in November 1970 while involved in the efforts to salvage and extinguish a blaze aboard the stricken oil tanker *Pacific Glory*. Six years earlier, another tug came to grief on the shores of the Isle of Wight when the Smit salvage tug *Witte Zee* was holed and foundered during the attempted rescue of a Dutch Liberty ship, ashore at Brook. In this view, taken at the Princes Landing Stage at Liverpool during July 1967, the *John Lamey* is seen alongside her older steam running mate, the *Marie Lamey* of 1922, with between them, showing distinctive twin inclined exhausts, another converted motor tug, the *Edith Lamey*, originally completed as a steamer in 1942. *Kenneth Wightman*

LANGTON
(11/1964) Alexandra Towing Co
172grt; 102ft 11in (31.37m) loa x 27ft 1in (8.25m) beam
W. J. Yarwood & Sons, Northwich
Oil 2SA 8-cyl by Crossley Bros, Manchester: 1,200bhp

Alexandra Towing continued to adhere to the successful formula of having the single-screw tug installed with Crossley diesels driving the main shaft through a single-reduction geared flexible coupling drive. Sister tugs of a broad class built to that configuration during the mid-1960s were the *Brockenhurst*, *Brocklebank*, *Egerton*, *Nelson*, *Romsey*, *Trafalgar*, *Ventnor* and the *Langton*, shown here. The *Langton* is seen on standby during July 1967, moored at the Princes Landing Stage at Liverpool, with (on her port side) the Mersey Docks & Harbour Board's steam tender *Vigilant*, a buoy, salvage and survey ship. *Kenneth Wightman*

NORTH ISLE

(4/1959) Alexandra Towing Co
200grt; 104ft 6in (31.85m) loa x
   28ft (8.53) beam
W. J. Yarwood & Sons, Northwich
Oil 2SA 8-cyl by Crossley Bros,
   Manchester: 1,350bhp

The *North Isle* was launched on 18 November 1958, entering service five months later with Alexandra Towing on the Mersey. As such she was first motor-driven tug to enter service with the company. The order for her construction had been largely influenced by the success with diesel propulsion enjoyed by the Red Funnel Towage company at Southampton, which had introduced its first motor tugs some three years earlier. In fact, Alexandra Towing used the same Crossley Bros eight-cylinder diesels adopted by Red Funnel, thereby giving their tugs the same horsepower. Although initially used on the Mersey, the *North Isle* was transferred to Southampton in February 1962 where she remained until September 1975, from which date she spent four years on station at Gibraltar. During November 1970 she attended, along with the *John Lamey*, the blazing oil tanker *Pacific Glory* in Sandown Bay, Isle of Wight. Here she is seen, around 1960, pulling a vessel in the Gladstone Dock with Canadian Pacific's 27,284-gross-ton *Empress of England* in the background. *Kenneth Wightman*

PEA COCK

(1/1960) North West Tugs Ltd
159grt; 95ft 3in (29.03m) loa x 25ft 11in
  (7.90m) beam
Cammell Laird & Co, Birkenhead
Oil 4SA 6-cyl by Ruston & Hornsby,
  Lincoln: 1,080bhp

The *Pea Cock* was the first of a trio of motor tugs which, unbeknown at the time, were the last tugs to be built for the North West Tugs company. They were derivatives of the earlier duo of motor tugs, namely the *Heath Cock* and *West Cock*, whose successful diesel propulsion had proved a real benefit in the confined waters of the Liverpool dock system. In 1966 North West Tugs was acquired by the Alexandra Towing Company and four years later the former 'Cock' tugs were re-christened with Alexandra names ie those of the Liverpool docks complex. Thus, the *Pea Cock* was renamed *Canada*. Here she is seen in her original North West Tugs livery in the lock, standing by to manoeuvre. In 1981 the *Canada* was sold to Nicolas E. Vernicos and renamed *Canada II*, soon altered to *Vernicos Georgis*. As such she was lost that October on passage to Greece while towing her former fleetmates *Heath Cock* and *Weather Cock* — see under the *Heath Cock* on page 56. *World Ship Society*

WEATHER COCK

(8/1960) North West Tugs Ltd
159grt; 95ft 3in (29.03m) loa x 25ft 11in (7.90m) beam
Cammell Laird & Co, Birkenhead
Oil 4SA 6-cyl by Ruston & Hornsby, Lincoln: 1,066bhp

The *Weather Cock* differed only marginally from her two sisters in that her Ruston & Hornsby diesels were coupled to a two-speed single-reduction and reverse gearing arrangement. Her completion marked the end of a three-year, five-tug building programme by Cammell Laird during a time when the yard enjoyed full order books. The *Weather Cock* was renamed *Formby* following her transfer to Alexandra Towing during 1966. For her ultimate fate, see the *Heath Cock* on page 56. In this view, taken on 3 October 1964, she is seen moored abreast of an unidentified Johnston Warren tug alongside the wharf of the Brocklebank Warehouse. *Jim McFaul*

WEST COCK

(3/1958) North West Tugs Ltd
193grt; 102ft 2in (31.14m) loa x 27ft 11in
  (8.51m) beam
Cammell Laird & Co, Birkenhead
Oil 4SA 6-cyl by Ruston & Hornsby, Lincoln:
  1,088bhp

Built as a sister to the *Heath Cock*, the *West Cock* was only the second motor tug to enter service with North West Tugs. In 1966 she was taken over by the Alexandra Towing Company and, during 1970, in keeping with the treatment of other 'Cock' tugs that had been acquired, she was renamed *Morpeth*. In 1981, along with three other former North West Tugs, she was sold to Nicolas E. Vernicos, but unlike the others she successfully completed the voyage to Greece. Renamed *Vernicos Giannis* she did not, however, survive for long, for on 9 August 1983 she sank while under tow off Iráklion, Crete, following a collision with a cargo vessel. In this view the *West Cock* is seen operating the stern line of Harrison Line's Liverpool-registered *Author* as the 8,915-gross-ton cargo ship is manoeuvred into the dock basin. *World Ship Society*

WILLOWGARTH

(10/1959) Rea Towing Co Ltd
230grt; 105ft (32.0m) loa x 28ft 5in (8.66m)
  beam
P. K. Harris (Shipbuilders), Appledore
2 x Oil 4SA 7-cyl by Ruston & Hornsby,
  Lincoln: 1,680bhp

The *Willowgarth* along with her sister
Hazelgarth were two of the most powerful
motor tugs on the Mersey in the 1960s. With
their twin diesels single-reduction geared via
a flexible coupling to a single screw, each
was capable of 24 tons bollard pull. The
Willowgarth was laid down in January 1959
and launched four months later, both tugs
entering service in the same season. From
the photograph, taken around 1960, Rea
Towing tugs appear to be the preferred
choice of Alfred Holt & Company as their
10,109-gross-ton Blue Funnel liner *Perseus*
is towed through the lock by the
Willowgarth, at the bow, with an older steam
consort taking up the stern line. Having
passed into the ownership of Cory Ship
Towage in 1970, the *Willowgarth* remained
in service in January 2000, albeit under a
different name, having been sold on three
times since 1986. She first went to
Makedonia II Shipping Company, Greece, as
the *Thisseas* and then, two years later, the
Thisseas Shipping Company acquired her. In
1989 she moved to Evifan Towage-Salvage
Shipping Company, also Greece, for whom
she was renamed *Kapetan Giannis*.
Kenneth Wightman

BRIGADIER

(2/1961) Cory Ship Towage (Clyde)
  Ltd
223grt; 110ft 2in (33.57m) loa x 28ft
  3in (8.61m) beam
George Brown & Co (Marine),
  Greenock
Oil 2SA 8-cyl by Crossley Bros,
  Manchester: 1,128bhp

With a few exceptions, the photographs that follow are part of a series taken by Kenneth Wightman at Gourock, on the Clyde Estuary, during September 1974.

The *Brigadier* was originally built for Steel & Bennie Tugs of Greenock and launched on 5 December 1960, entering service two months later. She was used primarily for harbour towage but could also operate on a coasting towage service. After transferring to Rea ownership in 1969, after Steel & Bennie was taken over, and subsequently to Cory Ship Towage, in whose colours she is seen here approaching Gourock harbour, she was briefly renamed *Forager* in 1976 in order to release the name *Brigadier* for a new vessel. Within the year she had changed ownership to Whitliff Corp (for whom A. & N. Vogel, London, was the manager) to become the *Fortrose*. During October of that same year she was operating at Loch Kishorn under charter to Howard Doris. In 1981 Soc Armamento Gestione Navigacione SrL of Sargenavi, Italy, acquired her and she was still in this company's service as of 2000, apparently without having had a further change of name. Sometime between 1970 and 1976 the *Brigadier* was substantially modified, having a modern wheelhouse constructed while twin inclined, flue-like exhausts replaced her single original funnel.
Kenneth Wightman

CAMPAIGNER

(1957) Cory Ship Towage (Clyde) Ltd
248grt; 114ft 1in (34.77m) loa x 29ft
   10in (9.09) beam
James Lamont & Co, Port Glasgow
Oil 2SA 8-cyl by H. Widdop & Co Ltd,
   Keighley: 1,065bhp

The single fixed-pitch screw, double-reduction geared *Campaigner* was launched for Steel & Bennie of Greenock on 30 July 1957, some 10 months after her keel was laid down. Mainly used for harbour towage, she could also be employed on coastal towing voyages. One of these occurred during April/May 1967 when she towed the former Light Vessel *Comet*, then operating as Radio Scotland, from Ballycote off Northern Ireland. The trip involved towing her charge around the north coast of Scotland, outside of territorial waters, to an anchorage beyond the Forth Estuary where Radio Scotland could resume broadcasting. By 1970 in the hands of Cory Ship Towage, she remained with these owners until 1977 when she was sold to Frank Pearce (Tugs) Ltd, Poole, and renamed *Pulwell Victor*. Four years later she was sold again, to Atrefs Shipping Company, Greece, becoming the *Marambu*. A third move, in 1984, took her to Kappa Maritime Company, Greece, for whom she remained in an active condition until August 2004 under the name *Kappa*. She was then broken up at Aliaga, Turkey. This view shows the *Campaigner* making her way out of Gourock harbour with prominent buildings of the town in the background. The line of cars on the quayside acts as a good indicator of the date of the photograph (1974). *Kenneth Wightman*

CHIEFTAIN

(1930) Cory Ship Towage (Clyde) Ltd
223grt; 113ft (34.44m) loa x 24ft 1in (7.34m)
  beam
Scott & Sons, Bowling
Oil 4SA 8-cyl by Klöckner-Humboldt-Deutz,
  Cologne: 660bhp

The *Chieftain* was launched as a steam driven tug on 27 March 1930 for Steel & Bennie Ltd of Greenock and in her original configuration sported the tall, natural-draught funnel of a steamer. She was converted to diesel propulsion in 1957 to update her with other motor tugs then being purchased by the towage company. After long service with Steel & Bennie and, subsequently, Cory Ship Towage, the *Chieftain* was sold to the Falmouth Towage Co and renamed *St Eval* for use as a harbour towage tug and to aid vessels entering and leaving the growing A&P ship repair yard located in the port. After some 57 years' service engaged in towage work she was withdrawn with the intention that she be used as a yacht trials accommodation vessel. However, this fell through and instead she went to the scrapyard during 1987. *Kenneth Wightman*

FLYING DEMON
(4/1964) Clyde Shipping Co, Glasgow
131grt; 92ft 6in (28.19m) loa x 23ft 7in
  (7.19m) beam
J. Lewis & Sons, Aberdeen
Oil 2SA 6-cyl by British Polar Engines Ltd,
  Glasgow: 1,140bhp

The introduction of the single controllable pitch propeller (CPP) along with a powerful British Polar engine made the *Flying Demon* one of the most manoeuvrable and powerful tugs for its size, having a bollard pull of 16 tons. Once the propeller's hydraulic system had been tuned to perfection, the benefits of CPP were soon realised for confined harbour work. She became the *Forth* in 1984, following her sale to Forth Tugs Ltd, Grangemouth, and two years later was sold again to Fowey Harbour Commissioners for whom she was renamed *Tregeagle*. At the time of writing she is believed to still be in service with these operators. This view, taken from the paddle steamer *Waverley*, shows her in July 1981 near Renfrew on the River Clyde. In the background is the *Lancaster*, the former Ellerman Lines ship *City of Lancaster*, laid up after sustaining collision damage, with beyond her, to the right, the tower of Renfrew town hall. *Kenneth Wightman*

FLYING DIPPER

(4/1958) Clyde Shipping Co, Glasgow
274grt; 113ft 10in (34.69m) loa x 29ft
  11in (9.12m) beam
A. & J. Inglis, Glasgow
Oil 2SA 7-cyl by British Polar Engines
  Ltd, Glasgow: 1,200bhp

The *Flying Dipper* was launched for the Clyde Shipping Co of Glasgow on 11 December 1957 as a development of the earlier *Flying Duck*, distinguishable by the longer side screens extending aft from her bridge. Her primary role was one of harbour towing and berthing assistance on the Clyde. While performing these duties, assisting Shaw Savill's *Doric* in Stephen's Basin on the River Clyde on 18 October 1966, she was struck and holed by the liner's propeller and sank. Fortunately, there was no loss of life. With the aid of the Admiralty tug *Succour*, she was raised that December, subsequently repaired and returned to service. Clyde Shipping sold her to Nautilus Continental Lines SA, Panama, in 1978 and she was renamed *Pamela Joy*. During the delivery voyage, bound from Hull to Kuwait, she suffered fire damage and was obliged to put into Lisbon. While there, on 21 July 1978, an engine room fire resulted in her sinking at her anchorage in the River Tagus. In the following month she was raised but being beyond repair she was broken up at Setubal, Portugal. *Kenneth Wightman*

FLYING DUCK
(10/1956) Clyde Shipping Co, Glasgow
176grt; 99ft (30.17m) loa x 26ft 11in (8.20m)
  beam
A. & J. Inglis, Glasgow
Oil 2SA 6-cyl by British Polar Engines Ltd,
  Glasgow: 1,075bhp

The *Flying Duck*, launched on 23 May 1956 for the Clyde Shipping Co of Glasgow, is here seen some 18 years later plying through the calm waters of the Clyde. She entered service on 29 October 1956 in the role of harbour towing and berthing assistance tug. Despite her smaller dimensions compared to some of her consorts, she could still manage a bollard pull of some 13.5 tons. In 1976 she was sold by Clyde Shipping to the Dundee Harbour Trustees and renamed *Scotscraig*. Moved to Dundee Harbour, she remained in operation there for 10 years until, in 1986, she was sold on again to C. W. Shipping Ltd of Limerick in the Irish Republic. Upon her transfer to the Irish tug company she was again renamed, *Shannon Estuary I*. She served her new owners until 1989 when it seems she was laid up indefinitely with surveys overdue. By September 1998 she was lying abandoned derelict at Cahiracon on the River Shannon. It was announced on 16 November 2000 that she was scheduled for demolition locally. However, during early 2005 it was reported that she remained in existence, still located at Cahiracon. *Kenneth Wightman*

FLYING FALCON
(2/1968) Clyde Shipping Co, Glasgow
213grt; 110ft 7in (33.71m) loa x 28ft 2in (8.59m) beam
James Lamont & Co, Port Glasgow
Oil 2SA 7-cyl by British Polar Engines Ltd, Glasgow: 1,470bhp

The tug *Flying Falcon* was launched for the Clyde Shipping Co on 4 October 1967, entering service five months later. She was designed for coastal service as well as harbour towage. Her engine exhausts were taken up through twin flue-type funnels which extended forward towards the mast, giving a tripod appearance. The *Flying Falcon* was later fitted with three fire-fighting nozzles, mounted on a tall tower to give optimum range when the water jets were in use. The *Flying Falcon* was sold in 1985 to Marine Transport Services in the Republic of Ireland. Renamed *Cathaigh*, six years later she was repurchased by her former owners, supposedly to revert to her original name. Within a year, however, she was resold to Tremos Maritime, a Honduran concern, and renamed *Demon*, changed to *Daimon* later in 1991. A further sale, the following year, took her to Greece under the name *Boukou L*. Ionian Marine Tugs Shipping converted the former *Flying Falcon* into a combined tug/cargo supply vessel before selling her on yet again in 1997 to another Greek operator. She was still in active service in October 2001. *Kenneth Wightman*

FLYING SPRAY

(9/1962) Clyde Shipping Co, Glasgow
184grt; 110ft 11in (33.80m) loa x 25ft 10in (7.87m) beam
Ferguson Bros, Port Glasgow
Oil 2SA 6-cyl by Nydqvist & Holm A/S, Trollhättan: 1,350bhp

The sister tugs *Flying Foam* and *Flying Spray*, laid down
respectively in November and December 1961 for the Clyde
Shipping Company, were both built locally by the same yard and
fitted with Swedish-manufactured Polar diesel engines. Their
flexible coupling drive and single-reduction reversing gear gave
them a high horsepower and made them ideal for harbour towage
and berthing duties. During 1974 they transferred under
management changes to Clyde Shipping (Tugs) Ltd of Glasgow.
In 1981 the pair were sold to the Italian company Medit SpA and
renamed *Nuvola Rossa* and *Nuvola Verde* respectively, continuing
to work together for the next 16 years. The association was broken
in 1997 when the former *Flying Foam* was sold to Rimorchiatori
Siciliani Srl of Palermo. The *Nuvola Verde* was also sold in October
2001 to ISE Srl, Trapani, Italy. As far as is known, both remain in
service. *Kenneth Wightman*

FLYING FULMAR

(2/1974) Clyde Shipping Co, Glasgow
298grt; 125ft 4in (38.21m) loa x 30ft 11in (9.43m) beam
Ryton Marine Ltd, Wallsend-on-Tyne
2 x Oil 4SA 6-cyl by British Polar Engines Ltd, Glasgow: 2,400bhp

Laid down in April 1972 and launched in July 1973, the *Flying
Fulmar* was not completed until February 1974 because of the
financial collapse of her builders, which led to her being
temporarily impounded. She was a development of the earlier
Flying Scout, and, like that tug, she was fitted with a single
controllable pitch propeller. Sold to Malcuth Srl, Italy, in June 1992
and renamed *Alce Nero*, en route to Palermo from Greenock she
towed her former fleetmate *Flying Scout*, purchased by the same
concern, which had been renamed *Aldebaran*. In May 1994 the ex
Flying Fulmar was sold again, to Rimorchiatori Siciliani, without
change of name. She was still in service in October 2001.
Kenneth Wightman

FLYING SCOUT

(2/1970) Clyde Shipping Co, Glasgow
290grt; 125ft 4in (38.21m) loa x
    29ft 11in (9.12m) beam
Scott & Sons (Bowling) Ltd
2 x Vee Oil 2SA 8-cyl by British Polar
    Engines Ltd, Glasgow: 2,400bhp

The single-controllable pitch screw *Flying Scout* was launched for the Clyde Shipping Co of Glasgow in July 1969. She was a slightly larger, updated version of the *Flying Falcon* featuring the same tripod mast and split funnels configuration. She was not only assigned for harbour and berthing duties but also intended for coastal towage work. In 1974 she transferred to the new management of Clyde Shipping (Tugs) Ltd. Twelve years later she was sold to Marine Transport Services Ltd, Cork, in May 1991 returning to Gourock under the ownership of Clyde (Holdings) Ltd. The following year she was disposed of to Malcuth Srl, as the *Aldebaran* (see under *Flying Fulmar*). A further sale to Rimorchiatori Siciliani Srl in 1996 brought another change of name, to *Leoncillo*. Under this name she was removed from Lloyd's Register in September 1996 because of overdue surveys. She languished for seven years and was finally scrapped in September 2003. The twin exhaust uptakes and mast 'tripod' arrangement can clearly be seen in this view at Gourock. Her near sister was the *Flying Fulmar*. *Kenneth Wightman*

VANGUARD
(4/1964) Cory Ship Towage (Clyde) Ltd
224grt; 110ft 2in (33.57m) loa x 28ft 3in (8.61m) beam
James Lamont & Co, Port Glasgow
Oil 2SA 8-cyl by Crossley Bros, Manchester: 1,122bhp

The main role of the *Vanguard*, which was launched on 26 February 1964 for Steel & Bennie of Greenock, was that of a tug/tender, permitting her to be used either for harbour towage or as a passenger tender for liners anchoring off Greenock. She was practically a sister, though a slightly modified version, of the company's earlier *Brigadier* with virtually the same tonnage, dimensions and single-reduction geared power plant. Both had a bollard pull of 13.5 tons. Following her work on the Clyde, the *Vanguard* was sold to Rocombe Shipping Ltd, Jersey, in 1981 but retaining her Glasgow registry. She was removed from Lloyd's Register in 1996 from which time her continued active operation, even existence, is doubtful. *Kenneth Wightman*

ATLAS

(7/1942) ex *Gele Zee* (1964) ex *Oceanus* (1953) ex *Christine
    Moller* (1951) ex *Frosty Moller* (1950) ex *Destiny* (1948)
    ex *USN BAT.9* Loucas Matsas & Sons, Piraeus
556grt; 143ft 6in (43.74m) loa x 33ft 3in (10.14m)
Defoe Shipbuilding Company, Bay City, USA
2 x Oil 2SA 12-cyl by General Motors Corp, connected to
    electrical motors: 1,875bhp

This much renamed and transferred motor tug started life as an American naval vessel, made available to Great Britain in wartime, along with 23 other similar craft, under the Lend/Lease arrangements. Employed as a rescue tug by the Royal Navy during World War 2, she was afterwards sold for mercantile salvage and towage operations with a variety of owners. Here the *Atlas* is shown, brightly painted, in the River Medway during June 1974. Twin-screwed, she was one of a relatively small number of tugs which had a diesel-electric engine installation. *Kenneth Wightman*

HERMES

(1956) Bugsier- Reederei und Bergungs AG,
   Hamburg

293grt; 126ft 4in (38.51m) loa x 27ft 4in (8.33m)
   beam

F. Schichau GmbH, Hamburg

2 x Oil 2SA 6-cyl by Klöckner-Humboldt-Deutz,
   Cologne: 1,900 ihp

Moored off Dover in July 1966 is the Bremerhaven-registered Bugsier tug *Hermes*. The famous Bugsier towage concern owned a large fleet of tugs ranging from small harbour tugs employed at the port of Hamburg as well as numerous ocean salvage tugs, the biggest in the early 1960s being the 1,093-gross-ton *Pacific*, completed in 1962. The *Hermes'* bridge is of an unusual glass-topped configuration, designed either to improve all-around visibility or as a means of allowing natural light to reach her bridge. The *Hermes* was renamed *Sea Queen* in 1976 when purchased by C. J. King & Sons (Tugs) Ltd, Bristol. *Kenneth Wightman*

KILLARNEY
(6/1919) ex *Unit Shipper* (1972) ex *Le Beau* (1970)
    ex *Haida Monarch* (1969) ex *S. D. Brooks* (1964)
    ex *St Faith* (1953) Unit Shipping Co (New Zealand)
    Ltd, Panama
422grt; 135ft 4in (41.24m) loa x 29ft 2in (8.89m) beam
Lytham Shipbuilding & Engineering Co Ltd
Oil 7-cyl by Fairbanks, Morse & Co, Chicago

This veteran tug, which has seen service with numerous owners in various parts of the world, was originally constructed as a steam-powered vessel for the Admiralty, one of the 48 vessels of the 'Saint' class of fleet tugs. Her reconditioned motor engines, fabricated in 1951, were installed in 1958 by her then owners, Kingcome Navigation Company, Vancouver. She makes an interesting comparison with other motor tugs in this book, having a distinctive, if not unique, profile. The *Killarney* is shown here as she appeared on 31 March 1977, moored in a busy, though unidentified, UK anchorage.
Kenneth Wightman

OCEANIC

(1968) Bugsier- Reederei und Bergungs AG,
  Hamburg
2,047grt; 286ft 2in (87.23m) loa x 48ft 6in
  (14.79m) beam
F. Schichau GmbH, Hamburg
2 x Oil 4SA 16-cyl by Klöckner-Humboldt-
  Deutz, Cologne

During a courtesy call to London in July 1969, the giant Bugsier salvage tug *Oceanic* is seen
berthed by Butlers Wharf in the Upper Pool. At the time she was probably the largest and most
powerful ocean-going tug in the world. Her twin engines drove controllable pitch propellers
through reduction gearing and hydraulic couplings. Butlers Wharf, on the Shad Thames
embankment, Bermondsey, opposite the entrance to the St Katharine Docks, was completed in
1873 and was then the largest warehouse complex on the Thames. It was an area associated with
the shipment into London of colonial and short-sea goods, typically large quantities of canned
produce, as well as sacked rice, coffee, tapioca and the like. Closed in 1972, it was left derelict for
some years but more recently it has been restored as a heritage site with cafés and art galleries.
Kenneth Wightman

STREMITELNIJ

(1957) Ministerstvo Ryibnogo Khazyaistva [Ministry of
    Fishing Operations], Kaliningrad, USSR
1,070grt; 201ft 8in (61.47m) loa x 37ft 9in (11.51m)
    beam
Valmet Øy, Åbo, Finland
Oil 2SA 5-cyl by MAN

The large Soviet, single-screw motor tug *Stremitelnij* (translated as 'Impetuous') paid a
call at London during October 1967, berthing in the Albion Dock, one of the nine large
enclosed docks comprising the Surrey Commercial Docks group. The *Stremitelnij* was
the lead-ship of a class of 21 ice-strengthened tugs of the *Orel* and *Kapitan Nokhrin*
types, all built in Finland. She was designated as a 'stand-by tug for the fishing fleet'
with the recognition number K 4-0606. At one time, however, she served as a rescue
tug with her hull painted black and the word 'SPASATEL' (meaning 'Rescue') printed
along her sides in white Cyrillic letters. *Kenneth Wightman*

TITAN
(1955) Bureau Wijsmuller, NV, Amsterdam
245grt; 104ft 11in (31.98m) loa x 27ft (8.23m) beam
C. V. Jonker & Stans, Hendrik-Ido-Ambacht
2 x Oil 2SA 8-cyl by N. V. Mach 'Bolnes', Bolnes:
   1,200bhp

By the time this picture was taken, in November 1963, the *Titan* was one of the smaller salvage tugs in the Wijsmuller fleet, the largest by then being the *Willem Barendz*, to be followed by a sister-tug, the *Jacob von Heemskerck*, in 1964. Wijsmuller was one of the big three ocean salvage companies, the others being Bugsier and, most famous of all, L. Smit & Company of Rotterdam. Unusually, the *Titan's* twin oil engines were geared to drive a single propeller shaft. Here she lies almost stationary in Gravesend Reach, the reason for her visit to UK waters not evident and unrecorded. Her sister tug, the *Cycloop*, was completed just under two years after her, in 1957. *Kenneth Wightman*

FAIRPLAY XI

(1963) ex *Aro* (1964) Fairplay Schleppdampf Reederei
GmbH, Hamburg
173grt; 99ft 5in (30.30m) loa x 24ft 10in (7.57m) beam
Schultz & Bruns, Emden
Oil SA 8-cyl by Klöckner-Humboldt-Deutz, Cologne:
1,750ihp

Here the Hamburg tug *Fairplay XI* is seen in the outer
reaches of the River Thames in October 1969, alongside
a pair of unidentified engines-aft general traders.
All three are displaying the internationally recognised
Collision Regulations (ColRegs) shape of a single black
ball, indicating that they are at anchor. At least one of the
two cargo vessels is also showing a quarantine flag. The
Fairplay XI was equipped with a 'directional' propeller,
making her highly manoeuvrable for work in restricted
dock areas. *Kenneth Wightman*

Front cover:
FLYING COCK

(2/1960) North West Tugs Ltd
165grt; 95ft 3in (29.03m) loa x 25ft 11in (7.9m) beam
Cammell Laird & Co, Birkenhead
Oil 4SA 6-cyl by Ruston & Hornsby, Lincoln:
1,080bhp

The *Flying Cock* was the last of a trio of tugs ordered
for North West Tugs Ltd. All were built by Cammell
Laird, as indeed had been the previous pair of motor
tugs for the company and, before that, some of its
earlier steam-driven tugs. As with her sisters *Pea Cock*
and *Weather Cock*, she had a single screw driven by
the main engine via a flexible coupling and single-
reduction and reversing gears. During 1966 North
West Tugs was acquired by Alexandra Towing. Four
years later, in 1970, the *Flying Cock* was renamed
Gladstone after the Liverpool dock of that name.
Here she is seen in her original North West Tugs
livery in tow of Clan Line's 6,454-gross-ton cargo
liner *Clan Mackintosh*. *World Ship Society*

Back cover:
VANQUISHER

(3/1955) Elliott Steam Tugs
294grt; 113ft 3in (34.52m) loa x 28ft 9in (8.76m)
beam
Henry Scarr Ltd, Hessle
Oil 2SA 8-cyl by British Polar Engines, Glasgow:
1,900 ihp

The *Vanquisher* in February 1967, long after she had
adopted the livery of the Ship Towage (London)
consortium. She continued, as did her fleetmates, to
operate on the River Thames after London Tugs passed
into the hands of Alexandra Towing in 1975. Her
career continued for another nine years with her new
owners until she was disposed of for scrap in 1984.
Kenneth Wightman

Bibliography and Sources
Blow Five by B. Hallam
(Journal of Commerce)
British Tugs by D. Ridley
Chesterton (Ian Allan),
4th and 5th editions
*Clyde Shipping Company,
Glasgow* by W. J. Harvey
and P. J. Telford
(P. J. Telford)
*Cory Towage Ltd — A Group
History* by W. J. Harvey
(World Ship Society)
Fifty Years of Naval Tugs by
B. Hannan (Maritime
Books)
Lloyd's Registers
Red Funnel & Before by
R. B. Adams (Kingfisher
Railway Productions)
United Towing 1920-1990 by
Alan Ford (Hutton Press)

Websites
www.clydesite.co.uk/
clydebuilt
www.english-heritage.org.uk
www.portcities.org.uk
www.tugtalk.co.uk
Tyne Tugs website at
lineone.net